The Systems Under My Bed

Dr. Federica Robinson-Bryant

The Systems Under My Bed

Published by Denotion Research Group
www.DenotionResearch.com

Cover & Illustrations by Tullip Studio

ISBN:
978-1-958634-40-0 (2nd edition print)
978-1-958634-19-6 (1st edition print)
978-1-958634-20-2 (eBook)

Printed in United States
2nd Edition

Dedication

This book is dedicated to the quiet
courage of believing in oneself.
May it remind you that among every battle,
seen or unseen, the truest victory is simply showing up
and doing your best, every time.

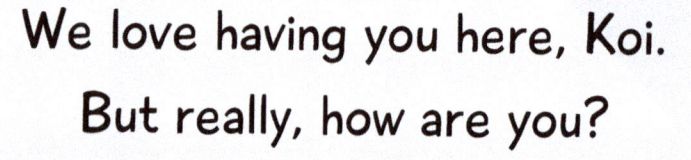

My mom taught me that no matter what you're going through, you must look for a light.

That mindset will fill you with enough courage and strength to put up a good fight.

One step at a time, Koi. Keep pushing and things will be fine. Stay positive and keep moving, and watch how everything else aligns.

You are creative, and you are strong!
You are smart, and you are sweet!
You are talented, amazing, and charming!
You are within yourself complete!

I see you and everyone who is helping.
I appreciate everything:
from the experiences I have tapped into to
the invaluable perspectives I have gained.

These systems are weaved into who we are,
filtering what we think, hear, know, and see.
It blurs others' view of who we are and what
we can do, and can either serve as weights
or springboards to dream.

When your school is tough or the environment is challenging, what will you achieve?

Always doing your best and rising through obstacles will help you to succeed.

Unexpected aid can come from people, places, and organizations, so you don't have to do it by yourself.

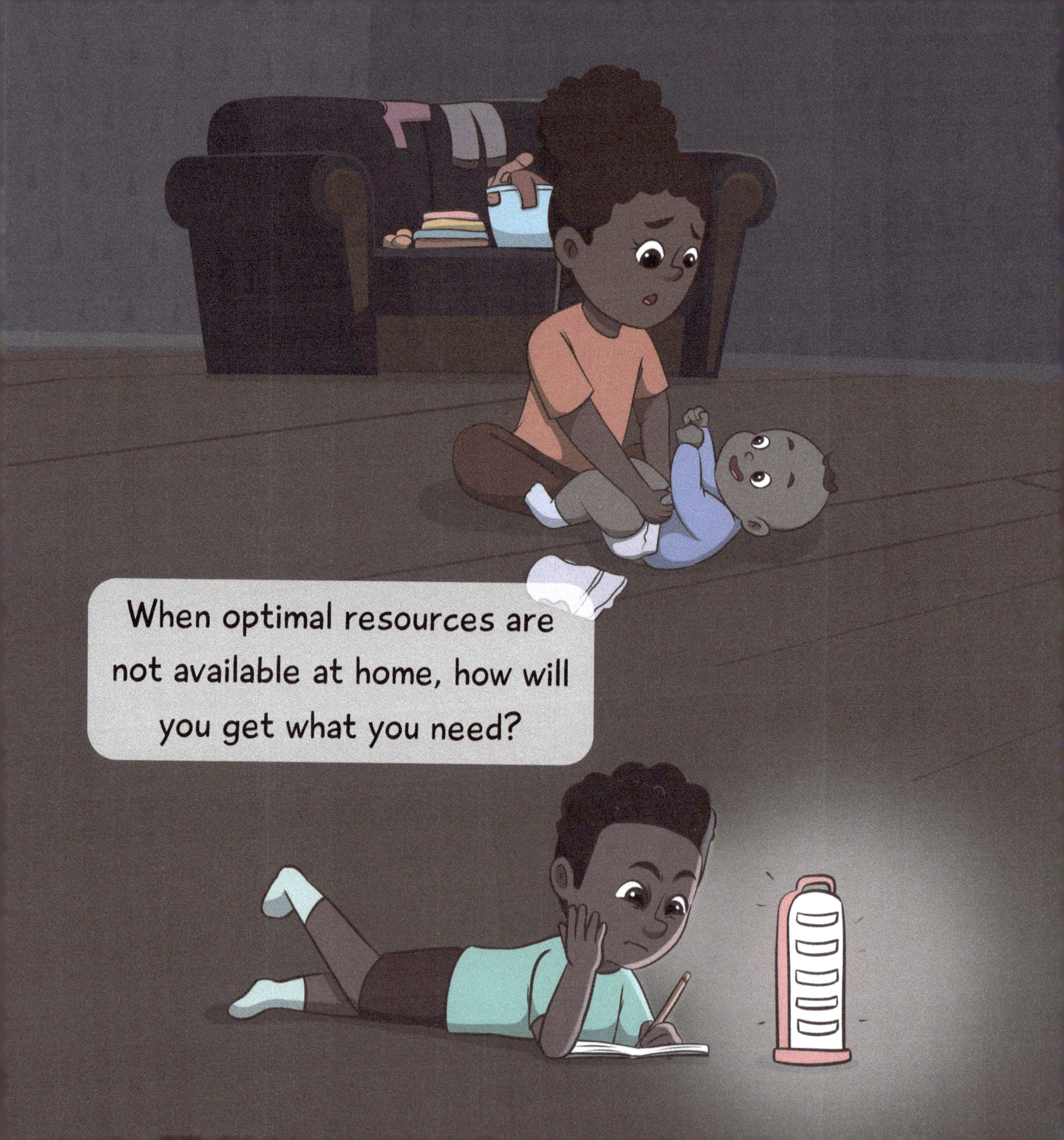
When optimal resources are not available at home, how will you get what you need?

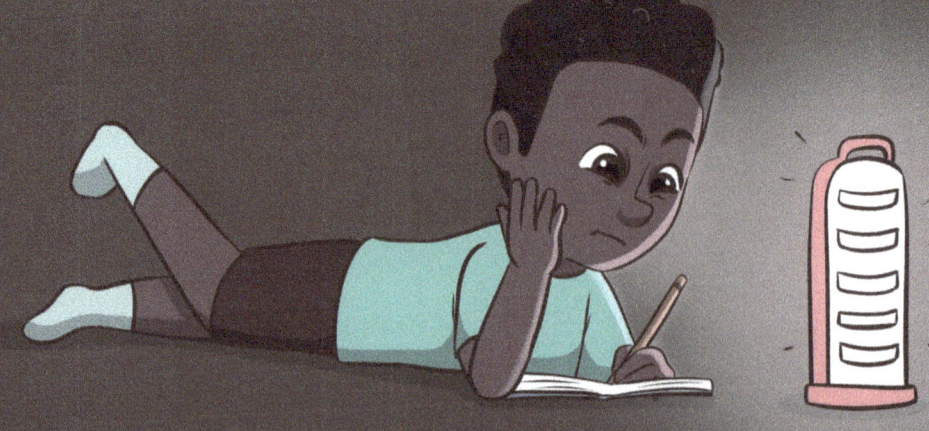

Sometimes alternatives can work out better than you ever thought, and are well within your reach.

Sometimes adapting means testing what you can do, and simply approaching things differently.

Sometimes creating means looking with fresh eyes, and letting your talents speak.

No matter what happens,
you can choose to be happy.
You can choose to continuously grow.
You can choose to be kind and ultimately
heal enough to open new doors.

Certainly, you cannot always control
the systems under your bed.
Their dusty and wicked webs will exist beyond you.
But you can choose to shine a flashlight upon the
darkness, to more clearly see the many paths and
options you could pursue.

PS: You've got this!

Vocabulary

Adapt

Align

Alternative

Barrier

Boundary

Challenge

Continuous

Control

Create

Different

Environment

Experience

Filter

Heal

Mindset

Opportunity

Optimal

Perceive

Persist

Perspective

Resource

Responsibilities

Sow

System

Vocabulary

- Test
- Uncertainty
- View

www.ingramcontent.com/pod-product-compliance
Lightning Source LLC
Chambersburg PA
CBHW041128120626

46547CB00019B/2905